Lingo Dingo
and the chef
who spoke Portuguese

Written by Mark Pallis
Illustrated by James Cottell

For my nieces - From Aunty Nathy

For Leo and Juniper - JC

For my awesome children - MP

LINGO DINGO AND THE CHEF WHO SPOKE PORTUGUESE

All rights reserved. This book or any portion thereof may not be reproduced or used in any manner whatsoever without the express written permission of the publisher except for the use of brief excerpts in a review.

Story edited by Natascha Biebow, Blue Elephant Storyshaping
First Printing, 2023
ISBN: 978-1-915337-90-0
MarkPallis.com

Lingo Dingo
and the chef
who spoke Portuguese

Written by Mark Pallis
Illustrated by James Cottell

NEU WESTEND
— PRESS —

This is Lingo. She's a Dingo and she loves helping.
Anyone. Anytime. Anyhow.

Lingo often helps her stylish neighbour Gunther, who lives by himself next door. She does a few jobs and has a nice chat. It makes Gunther feel good and it makes Lingo feel good too.

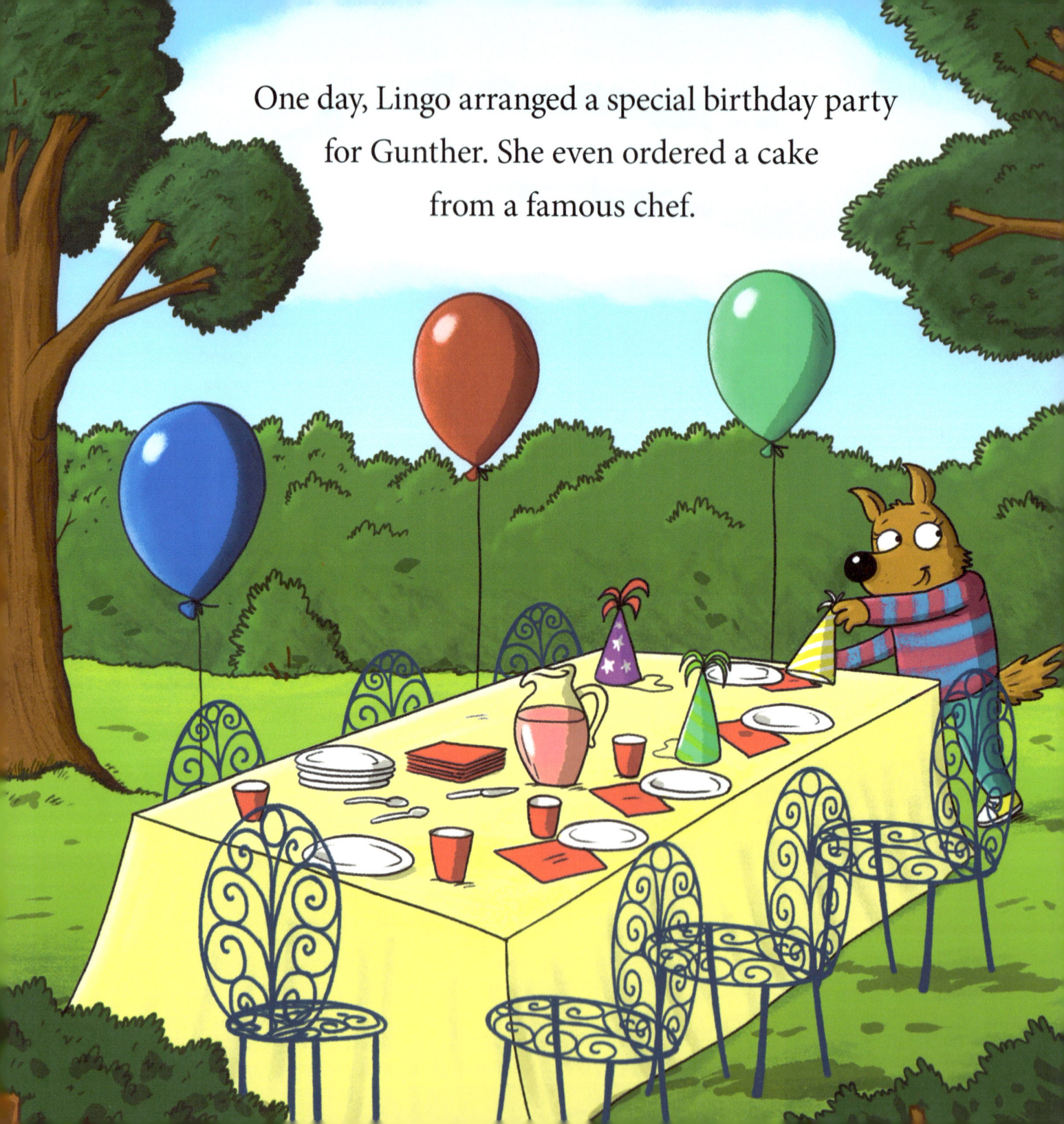
One day, Lingo arranged a special birthday party for Gunther. She even ordered a cake from a famous chef.

There was a knock at the door, "It must be the cake!" said Lingo. But it was a monkey.

"Olá. Sou o Chef Nono. Eu tenho um problema," he said.

Oh no. I can't speak Portuguese yet, thought Lingo. Maybe 'Olá' is like 'Hello'.

Olá = Hello; **Sou o / sou a** = My name is (masc/fem);
Eu tenho um problema = I have a problem

"Olá," said Lingo. Chef Nono replied slowly, "Lamento, mas não vou poder fazer o bolo de aniversário."

"I don't understand," said Lingo. "But let me guess. You want…"

Lamento = I am sorry; **mas não vou poder fazer** = I cannot make; **bolo de aniversário** = the birthday cake

"O meu forno está avariado," explained Chef.
"Posso usar o teu forno?"

Chef's oven must be broken thought Lingo. "I know! Let's bake the cake together," she said.

O meu forno está avariado = my oven is broken;
Posso usar o teu forno? = can I use your oven?

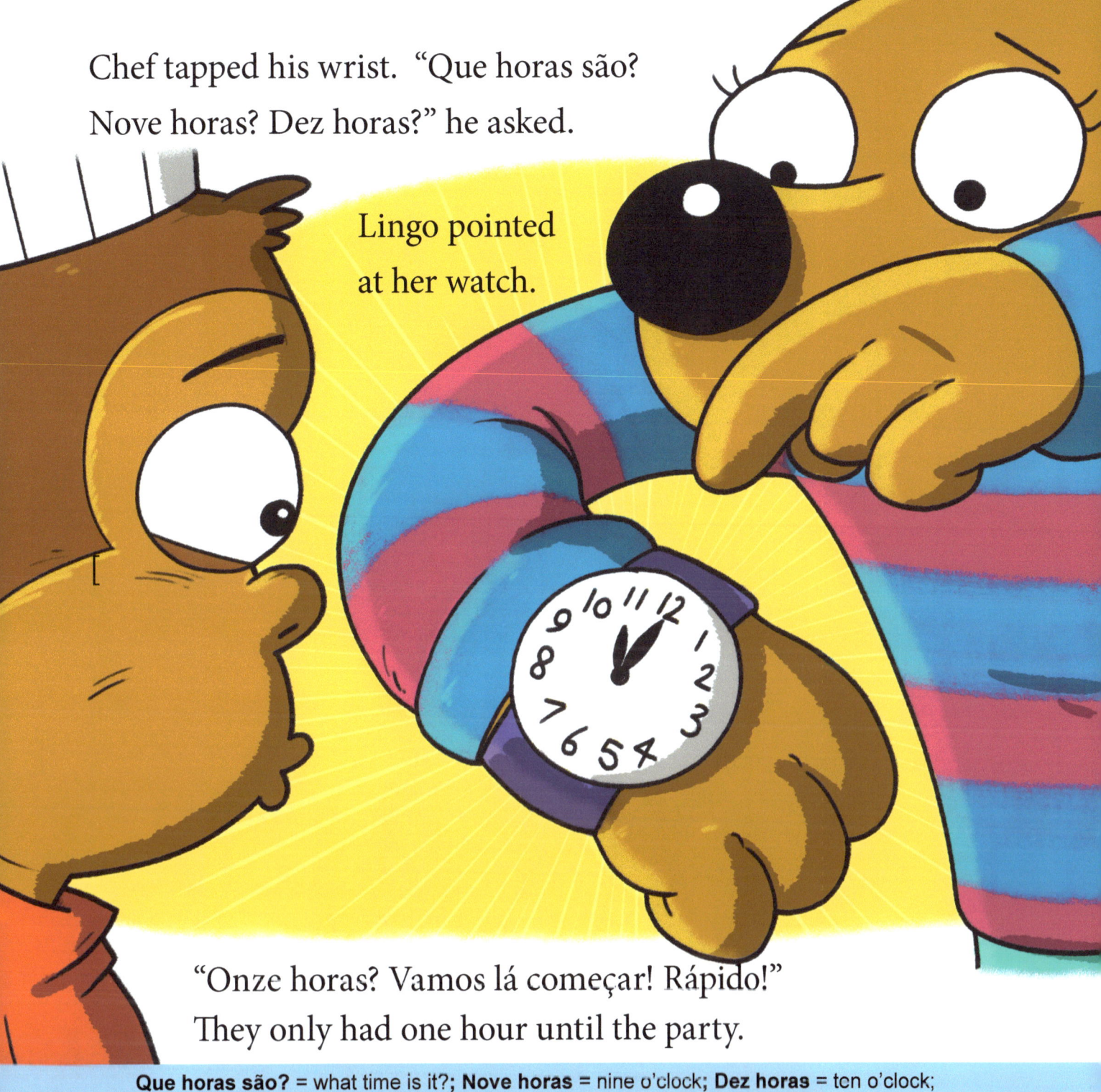

Chef tapped his wrist. "Que horas são? Nove horas? Dez horas?" he asked.

Lingo pointed at her watch.

"Onze horas? Vamos lá começar! Rápido!" They only had one hour until the party.

Que horas são? = what time is it?; **Nove horas** = nine o'clock; **Dez horas** = ten o'clock; **Onze horas?** = eleven o'clock; **Vamos lá começar!** = let's go; **Rápido!** = quick

Chef Nono and Lingo whizzed around the kitchen:

Um avental para ti = an apron for you; **Uma batedeira** = a whisk;
Uma tigela = a mixing bowl

"Por favor, dá-me a manteiga, o açúcar, os ovos e a farinha," said Chef.

Lingo wasn't sure what those words meant, so she just grabbed fish, coffee and onions instead.

"Peixe, café e cebola. Que nojo!" laughed Chef.

dá-me = pass me; **a manteiga** = the butter; **o açúcar** = the sugar; **os ovos** = the eggs; **e a farinha** = and the flour; **Por favor** = please; **Peixe** = fish; **café** = coffee; **cebola** = onions; **Que nojo** = disgusting

Chef plopped sugar, butter, eggs and flour into a bowl. "So that's what 'manteiga, açúcar, ovos e farinha' means!" laughed Lingo.

"Eu misturo, tu misturas, nós misturamos," said Chef and together they began to mix the cake.

Eu misturo = I mix; **tu misturas** = you mix; **nós misturamos** = we mix

"Finalmente, fermento em pó. Duas colheres," said Chef. Lingo guessed 'fermento em pó' meant baking powder, but how much?

Before she could ask, Chef hurried away, saying, "Com licença, eu preciso fazer xixi."

Lingo laughed, "I can guess what 'xixi' means!"

Finalmente = finally; **fermento em pó** = baking powder; **duas colheres** = two spoonfulls; **Com licença** = excuse me; **eu preciso fazer xixi** = I need to do a wee wee

I wonder if this is too much? thought Lingo as she added ten spoonfulls of 'fermento em pó' to the mix.

She carefully put everything into the oven and before long, a sweet cakey smell filled the kitchen.

fermento em pó = baking powder

"O que aconteceu? Está enorme," said Chef.

Lingo realised she had added too much baking powder.
"Sorry," she said sheepishly.

O que aconteceu? = what happened; **Está enorme** = it's huge

They somehow got the cake out of the oven but ...

it was so big ...

... they couldn't hold it. "Disaster!" cried Lingo. "Que desastre!" wailed Chef.

Que desastre! = what a disaster

"I know what will make you feel better," said Lingo, kindly. "Eat this ' cornichão'!"

"Que nojo. Odeio cornichões." said Chef.

They were running out of time.

Que nojo = disgusting; **Odeio cornichões** = I hate pickles

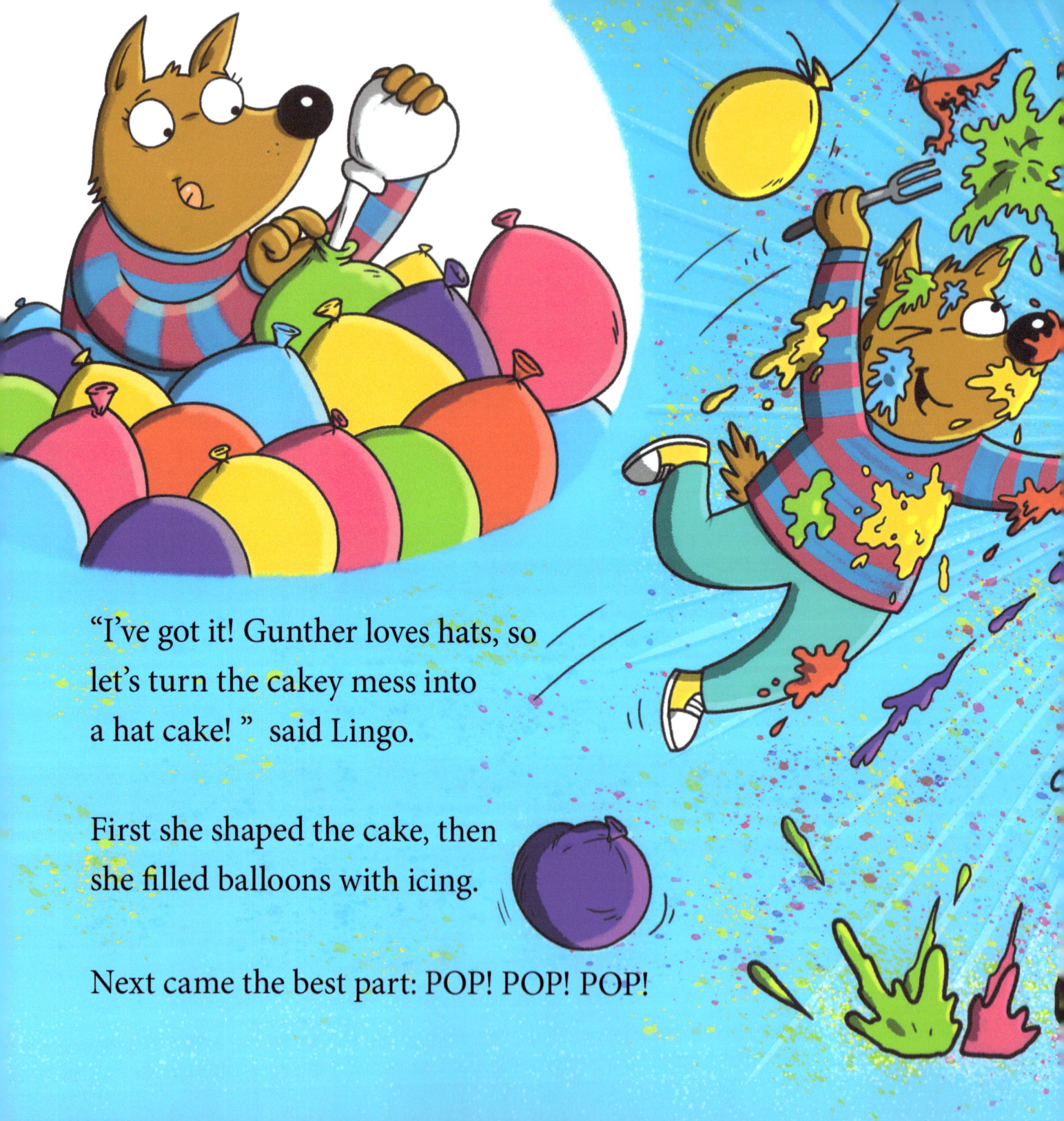

"I've got it! Gunther loves hats, so let's turn the cakey mess into a hat cake!" said Lingo.

First she shaped the cake, then she filled balloons with icing.

Next came the best part: POP! POP! POP!

It was a messy job but in the end, the cake looked fantastic. "Vermelho, laranja, amarelo, verde e azul. Fantástico!" said Chef.

vermelho = red; **laranja** = orange; **amarelo** = yellow;
verde = green; azul = blue; **Fantástico** = fantastic

There was a knock at the door. "A porta!" said Chef. It was Gunther, and he was wearing his special hat!

"Thankyou. This makes me feel so special," said Gunther. "You are special," replied Lingo.

A porta = the door

Gunther was thrilled with his cake.

Chef's deep voice sang "Parabéns a você..."

Parabéns a você = happy birthday / congratulations to you

"Sopra!" said Chef.

Gunther blew out all the candles in one puff and everyone tucked in.

sopra = blow

"Eu como, tu comes, ele come, ela come, eles comem," laughed Chef.

"Nós comemos !" added Lingo proudly.

Eu como = I eat; **tu comes** = you eat; **ele come** = he eats;
ela come = she eats; **eles comem** = they eat; **nós comemos** = we eat

Lingo, Gunther and Chef watched the sun go down.

"Eu estou feliz,
tu estás feliz.
Estamos todos felizes!" said Chef.

Eu estou feliz = I am happy; **tu estás feliz** = you are happy; **Estamos todos felizes!** = we are all happy

Baking a cake, helping a friend, learning a new language... what a day!

But now it was time for bed. It was time to dream about all the fun things that might happen tomorrow.

Learning to love languages

An additional language opens a child's mind, broadens their horizons and enriches their emotional life. Research has shown that the time between a child's birth and their sixth or seventh birthday is a "golden period" when they are most receptive to new languages. This is because they have an in-built ability to distinguish the sounds they hear and make sense of them. The Story-powered Language Learning Method taps into these natural abilities.

How the Story-powered language learning Method works

We create an emotionally engaging and funny story for children and adults to enjoy together, just like any other picture book. Studies show that social interaction, like enjoying a book together, is critical in language learning.

Through the story, we introduce a relatable character who speaks only in the new language. This helps build empathy and a positive attitude towards people who speak different languages. These are both important aspects in laying the foundations for lasting language acquisition in a child's life.

As the story progresses, the child naturally works with the characters to discover the meanings of a wide range of fun new words. Strategic use of humour ensures that this subconscious learning is rewarded with laughter; the child feels good and the first seeds of a lifelong love of languages are sown.

For more information and free learning resources visit www.neuwestendpress.com

You can learn more words and phrases with these hilarious, heartwarming stories from NEU WESTEND PRESS

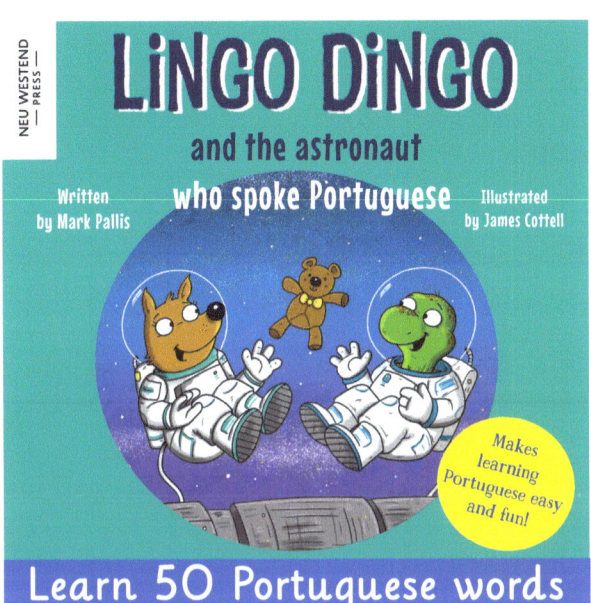

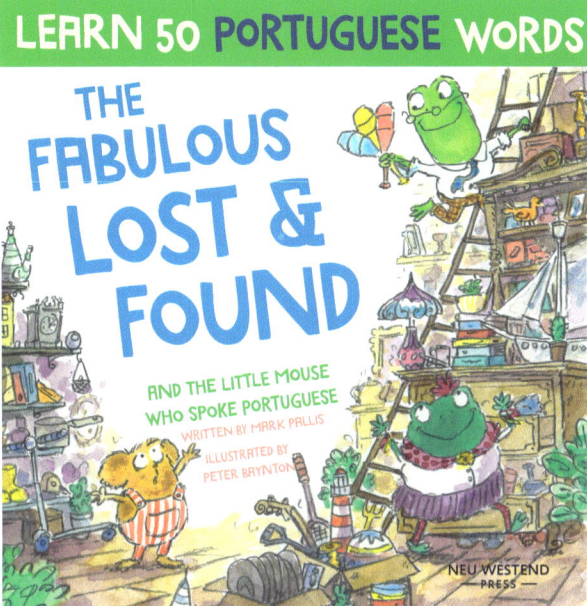

@MARK_PALLIS on twitter
www.markpallis.com

To download your FREE certifcate, and more cool stuff, visit
www.markpallis.com

@jamescottell on INSTAGRAM
www.jamescottellstudios.co.uk

> "I want people to be so busy laughing, they don't realise they're learning!"
> Mark Pallis

Crab and Whale is the bestselling story of how a little Crab helps a big Whale. It's carefully designed to help even the most energetic children find a moment of calm and focus. It also includes a special mindful breathing exercise and affirmation for children. Also available in French as 'Crabe et Baleine.'

Featured as one of Mindful.org's 'Seven Mindful Children's books'

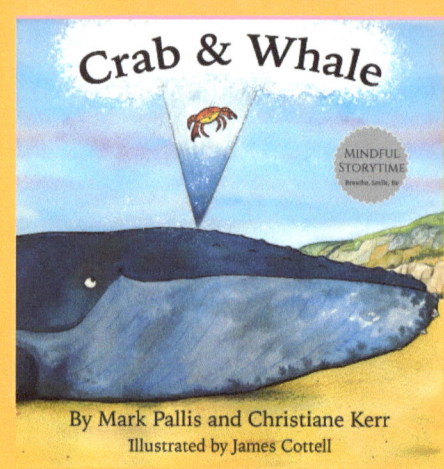

Do you call them hugs or cuddles?

In this funny, heartwarming story, you will laugh out loud as two loveable gibbons try to figure out if a hug is better than a cuddle and, in the process, learn how to get along.

A perfect story for anyone who loves a hug (or a cuddle!)

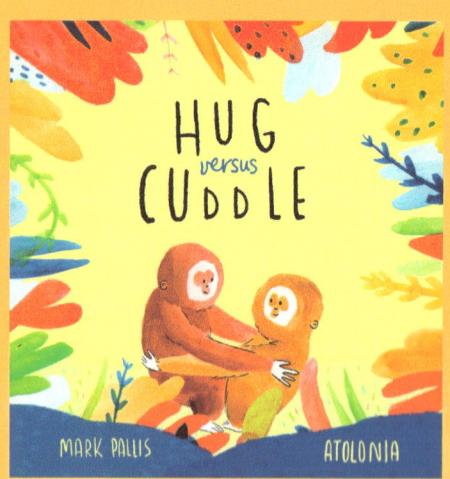

www.markpallis.com

www.ingramcontent.com/pod-product-compliance
Lightning Source LLC
Chambersburg PA
CBHW040020130526
44590CB00036B/41